Printed in China. Published by Leisure Time Press, 27259 Prescott Way, Temecula CA 92591   www.leisuretimepress.com

First Edition

Library of Congress Control Number 2013903216

Library of Congress Cataloging in Publication Data
McMahon, Jeff
Swimming to the moon - a collection of rhymes without reason

ISBN 978-0-9890270-0-7

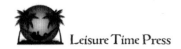 Leisure Time Press

To Janet, Greg and Shannon...

just because.

Swimming to the Moon

A Collection of Rhymes Without Reason

By Jeff McMahon

Art by Jessica Warrick

Leisure Time Press

My Super-Suction Shoes

I finally think I got it right,
lord knows I paid my dues.
I'm very pleased
to demonstrate
my super
suction-shoes.

They let you walk
on walls like
Spiderman for Halloween.
They're really very powerful
and you'll see what I mean.

It's just so darn exciting, but
I can't help that I'm feeling
a little dizzy since I wound up
stuck here on the ceiling.

I Once Fell Up The Stairs

It almost seems unnatural,
you wouldn't think you could
and I don't think it will ever be repeated
(knock on wood).

But my father saw it happen,
and he told me so and swears,
that he thought the world turned upside down,
when I fell up the stairs.

I was running to my bedroom
and my foot hit the first stair,
and before I knew what happened
I was flying through the air.

Although technically I don't think
flying's really what I did.
It was more like spazzy somersaults
and tumbling, with a skid.

But despite the laws of gravity
that should have made me stop,
I flipped and rolled right up the stairs
and made it to the top.

And I have no explanation,
it was all a bit surreal,
and it only took a week or two
for the bruises all to heal.

But my dad is my eyewitness
so if anybody cares,
I am in the Guinness Record Book
for falling up the stairs.

Under All This Dirt

I took a tumble in the dirt.
Well tumble's not the word.
I took a bath in piles of dirt,
that's really what occurred.

It covered my whole face
and body, and my clothes as well.
I think it covered everything
as far as I could tell.

And I decided it would be
an interesting test
to see if mom would know it's me,
and then I'd be impressed.

So I went home and rang the bell
as if I was a guest.
She opened up the door and then
she seemed a little stressed.

She made a kind of funny sound
and I could tell, indeed,
she couldn't tell if I was human
or a tumbleweed.

And I just stood there silently
still playing out my joke.
I thought she might go call the cops
and that is when I spoke.

And so I had to say to her
"it's me, your little squirt".
She really didn't recognize me
under all this dirt.

But once she heard my voice
she knew the dirty boy was me,
and now I'm in the bathtub
so I guess the joke's on me.

Free Throws

I walked to the line
and I sized up the shot.
They call it a free throw
but really it's not.

I just made a bet
for a five dollar bill.
He said I won't make it.
I said that I will.

So I shot the ball
just as smooth as I could.
The arc was just right and
rotation was good.

The ball started in
but instead rattled out.
It cost me five dollars
of that there's no doubt.

So this is the lesson
this bet taught to me.
Although they're called free throws
they're not always free.

Rise and Shine

When I wake up in the morn I've got
the rising part just fine
but I'm grumpy and dumpy and generally schlumpy
so I'm working on my shine.

Jail

They told me if I just skipped school for a day
a policeman could actually lock me away
and even though it didn't seem like a crime
they said that I'd soon find myself doing time.

I'd be thrown in the slammer, the hoosegow, the tank
and for just playing hooky, not robbing a bank
I'd be tossed in the joint and they'd lock me away
I'd be sent up the river with three squares a day.

The pokey, the prison, the cooler, the clink
a life behind bars is much worse than you think
I'd be locked in the big house, they'd throw out the key
they would put me on ice and I'd never be free.

And long after my friends had all graduated
I'd be in the calaboose, incarcerated
and they'd live their lives, moving on, being free,
while I'm stuck in the penitentiary.

And life at the rock would have all kinds of rules
and I'd think back in fondness of my days in school
so maybe I'll rethink the plan that I had
cause compared to these options my school's not so bad.

This Is Not The Way It Goes

We're making lots of progress
but there's things that I oppose,
so I feel I must inform you
this is not the way it goes.

I knew it when we started this
it didn't seem quite right.
Certain parts were way too loose
and some were much too tight.

And things that should have been on top
were winding up below,
and all the little doo-dads
didn't have a place to go.

And the thingamabob was all bent out of shape,
and the watchamacallit was too,
and the part on the front should have been on the back
where the wires go all the way through.

We lost the instructions five hours ago,
so now we are really just faking.
I honestly haven't the slightest idea
of what we're supposed to be making.

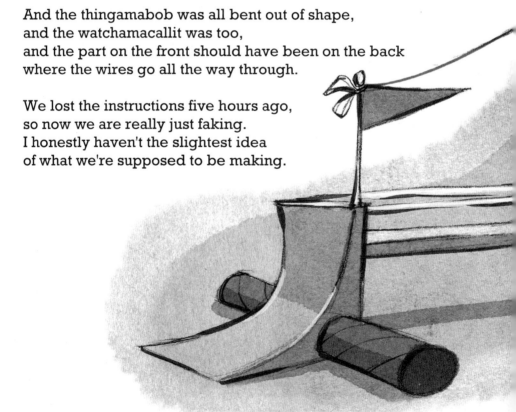

My Shadow Gave Me A Dirty Look

My shadow gave me a dirty look,
the reason, I suppose,
is everywhere we go I'm always
stepping on its toes.

The Dresser

I must admit, I'm quite impressed.
Why, just the other day,
my little brother got all dressed.
Well almost, anyway.

His shoes were on the wrong feet
and his socks were inside out.
His jeans were pulled on backwards
and his belt was turned about.

And once he got his shirt on, well,
he kind of looked a wreck.
His head was in the armhole
and one arm was out the neck.

But he clearly made the effort
and deserves another chance.
It can't be easy pulling
underwear over your pants.

So I give him lots of credit
'cuz he obviously tried,
but I'm glad I got a glimpse of him
before he went outside.

The Shopping Cart Adventure

We had quite an adventure
at the grocery store today
with my little sister still inside
our cart just got away.

My mother wasn't certain
what preceded the event
but she turned to grab a can of corn,
let go, and off it went.

She saw it start to roll and tossed
the corn back on the shelf.
She tried to grab and missed
and watched the cart just steer itself

past the yogurt, past the cheese
past the lettuce, past the peas
past the onions, past the chives
past the" cleanup - aisle five"
past the ketchup, past the pickles
past the freezer with popsicles.

Mom was screaming "Stop that cart"
running round the super mart
and that cart was moving fast
within seconds it had passed

cans on sale, due to dents
lemons, five for fifty cents
past the soda, past the juice
past two toddlers running loose
past some specials on a table
past a lady reading labels
dodging shoppers, passing carts
causing flailing body parts

(my sister hadn't whined or cried.
I think she thought it was a ride)

the cart was not inclined to stop
until it hit a pail and mop
for it had circled and arrived
back at that mess in aisle five.

And looking back I was impressed
that shopping cart was quite possessed.
It rolled around like it was knowing
where it wanted to be going
as if some unknown ghostly force
was driving 'round this shopping-course

but when it all was said and done
no one was hurt and sis had fun
and mom recovered from her state
(she's known to hyperventilate).

I told my mom to tell me when
she's going to the store again.
I hope I can tell them apart
I really want that shopping cart.

Sticks And Stones
and Broken Bones

Sticks and stones can break your bones
and names can never hurt you.
But since Bob's Diner's sign fell down
I'm not so sure that's true.

Juice Box

I had a little juice box and
it had a little straw
I gave a little squeeze and
I found a little flaw.

I meant to take a little sip
but little did I know
it only takes a little squeeze
and juices start to flow.

A juice box may be little
but it packs a lot of juice
and it doesn't take much pressure
from a squeeze to turn it loose.

So I learned a little lesson
and I'll gladly share the tip.
It's once you poke the straw inside
you do not squeeze, you sip.

I Don't Have Time To Sleep

With everything that's going on
here in my tiny town
I find myself with things to do
before the sun goes down.

And as the dusk approaches
and the evening stars come out,
there's oh so much I haven't done
that we should talk about.

I haven't built a rocket
and I haven't dug a moat,
thrown my sister in the swimming pool
to see if she can float.

And I never ever even
had a gremlin for a pet.
Though I think I might be getting one
I haven't got it yet.

And I didn't eat an insect
on a plate or on a bun.
(Oh alright I ate a bug once,
but for money, not for fun).

And no one really seems concerned
about these things I've missed.
There's just so much I haven't done
I need to keep a list.

I didn't do my homework,
didn't take the garbage out,
or several hundred other things
my parents yell about.

So even though I'd like to do
the things that seem like fun
the homework and the garbage
are the things that must get done.

And when I do the things I should
there's so much that I've missed.
I never seem to get to do
the fun things on my list.

Like making milk shakes out of mud,
Or noodles a la mode.
Put marshmallows in the microwave
to see if they'll explode.

Or mix sugar with the salt
so it will come out salty-sweet.
Or fill my shoes with jello so
they're squishy on my feet.

And with so much stuff to do
it's just impossible to keep
ahead of things and that is why
I don't have time to sleep.

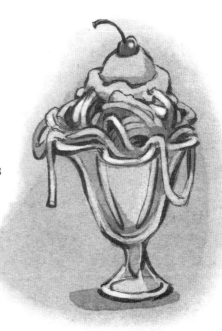

So don't set my alarm clock
or you'll waste it's noisy beep.
With all that I have yet to do
I don't have time to sleep.

And while other kids are in their beds
so sweetly counting sheep
because their parents told them to,
I don't have time to sleep.

I know it's after midnight
so I will not make a peep,
but I'm just now getting started and
I don't ...have...time...to...zzzzz.

Snoozin' Susan

Snoozin' Susan is sound asleep,
but somehow her hand and her arm,
continue to press, with tremendous success,
the snooze button on her alarm.

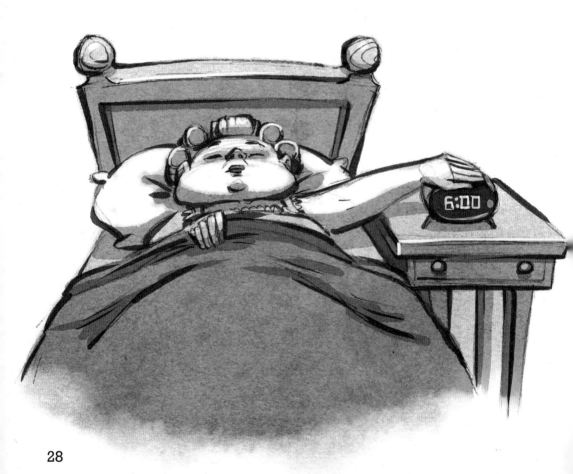

Hot Trick

To keep my cup of cocoa warm
I learned this from a poster.
Before you put your cup down, put
your coasters in the toaster.

Rocket Pilot

I'd like to fly a rocket and
I'm sure I'm qualified.
You just put on your spacesuit,
pop the hatch, and go inside
and settle in the captain's chair
that's where you will reside
and then you check the instruments
(each button should be tried)
and maybe then you start to read
the pilot how-to guide
(that's something I'm assuming that
the rocket folks provide)
and once I've done my reading
and my knowledge is applied
I'll point my rocket at the moon
and just enjoy the ride.

Now there are those who say my plan
is oversimplified.
There's things in space most every place
with which you can collide
like meteors and asteroids
and there's no place to hide
it's actually quite dangerous
that cannot be denied
so when I said I'm qualified
I guess I kind of lied
and rather than pretending
I've done things I've never tried
I'm better off not taking off
and swallowing my pride.
I'll leave the flights to astronauts
and I'll just go outside
and watch the heavens from the earth
content and starry-eyed.

After You

We went to see a movie at the theater Sunday night,
and I figured I'd surprise you and be perfectly polite.

I got to the door first and then I knew just what to do.
I held the door wide open and I stated "after you".

I got into the ticket line as gentlemen should do.
I offered you my place in line and I said, "after you".

I got in the refreshment line to get a snack or two,
but let you go in front of me and uttered "after you".

And as I stepped aside I bumped a guy with a tattoo.
He dumped his popcorn everywhere and spilled his Mountain Dew.

It seemed my safest option was to turn around and flee.
I guess good manners do not pay, 'cause now he's after ME.

Black And Blue
is Nothing New

Black and blue is nothing new,
we're very well acquainted.
When people see how bruised I am
well, some of them have fainted.

My knees and elbows, shins and wrists,
are all both black and blue.
My shoulders, knuckles, heels and neck
are all that color too.

What I must say, in my defense,
is that they should require
a warning label on the door -
DO NOT PLAY IN THE DRYER!

The Paperboy

The paperboy on my street needs
to work on how he throws.
It's sometimes in the bushes,
some days who knows where it goes.

Today he threw it on the roof
that dirty little louse,
although I didn't have to pay
he said it's on the house.

Kitchen Dares

I'm working on some recipes
but not the normal kind
the ones that I am working on
I doubt you'd ever find.

Vanilla in my mashed potatoes
jelly in my soup
and a handful of garbanzo beans
served in an ice cream scoop

peanut butter onions and
banana flavored peas
and chocolate covered broccoli
with mozzarella cheese

and how about a salad
with some licorice whips and ice
and a baked potato sundae would sure
top it off real nice.

It's only the beginning
of the menu I'd create
but please don't ever ask me to
put all this on my plate.

Shoes Are Gloves For Feet

I made a cool discovery,
it's something really neat.
It came to my attention that
your shoes are gloves for feet.

They do both have their differences
and here's a few of those:
While gloves have separate fingers,
shoes don't separate the toes.

And given that your hands
are usually washed after they touch
something dirty, slick or smelly,
gloves don't tend to stink as much.

Your shoes now, on the other hand,
(I should say other foot),
can taint the breeze like stinky cheese,
no matter where they're put.

So gloves don't tend to have offensive
odors like a shoe.
And shoes will never get the chance
to pick a nose or two.

And there are similarities,
for instance in a storm,
if shoes and gloves are waterproof,
they'll keep things dry and warm.

They're similar yet different;
they don't need to compete.
So keep your hands inside your gloves
and shoes upon your feet.

April May June

April May June, she was born in July
and by August the doctors all thought she would die
'cause she ate all the forks and she swallowed a spoon.
There's quite a collection in
April May June.

Now April May June it was clear was quite ill
and for spoon and fork eating there isn't a pill.
All the doctors were sure that the end would come soon
for the silverware-swallowing
April May June.

But our April May June she just didn't agree
and she sat up in bed and she counted to three
and she burped and she belched from that morning 'til noon,
our dear dinnerware-upchucking
April May June.

And now April May June seems she's just good as new
even though all the experts were sure she was through,
so now watch what you eat is the name of that tune,
and don't leave utensils near
April May June.

Dance Lessons

Be careful, if you get the chance
to teach an elephant to dance.
Be sure to mind your P's and Q's
but mostly mind your toes and shoes.

Dan Ticipation

Dan Ticipation was running for mayor
the votes had just now been collected,
and all the excitement was starting to build
to see who was really elected.

So we're sitting around on the edge of our seats
and it's building up great expectation
while we wait for the answer and all hold our breath
as we're waiting with Dan Ticipation.

Driving Doesn't
Seem So Hard

I've given this a lot of thought
while sitting in my yard
and I've come to the conclusion
driving doesn't seem so hard.

Now here's the way I see it
from the studying I've done.
It isn't like it's rocket science
to get the car to run.

You open the door
you get inside
you put in the key
and get ready to ride.

Adjust the mirrors
adjust the seat
make sure that the pedals
are reached by your feet.

Roll down the windows
and crank up the tunes
keep both your eyes open
for cats and raccoons.

Rest your very best sunglasses
up on your head
and tell me once more
why we need driver's ed.

I've been driving forever
although I'm just eight
sure it's video games
but my scores have been great.

So I think that I'm ready
to give it a go.
People say that I'm too young
but what do they know.

But I do have two questions
before matters get worse.
Which way is forward
and which is reverse?

The Escalator Broke

I was minding my own business
riding calmly to the top
when I heard a little thump and then
we grinded to a stop.

I hope they called the maintenance guys,
I haven't got all day.
I hadn't really planned on a
mechanical delay.

They didn't post procedures or
evacuation plans.
I guess I have to wait right here
and leave it in their hands.

I pray this problem's being fixed
I'm getting kind of scared.
I guess I could be here all night
if this is not repaired.

At first I found it funny
but by now it's not a joke.
I'm having trouble breathing
since the escalator broke.

It seems they should have notified
the firemen and police.
I don't think they can fix this with
a hammer and some grease.

They need to call a specialist
familiar with the task.
I'd like to see the National Guard.
Is that too much to ask?

My hands are getting sweaty
and my legs are getting numb.
I'm sure that help is coming
but I don't know where it's from.

I'm feeling kind of dizzy
but it seems like no one cares.
The escalator choice was bad,
I should have used the stairs.

Snizzles

Snizzles are sneezes
that aren't fully grown
kind of like sniffles
but not as well-known
they float all around us
and kind of lay low
then fly up your nose
when they're ready to blow.

Tree Climbing 101

I've got a course that's lots of fun.
It's called Tree Climbing 101.
It's for beginners, obviously,
who never, ever climbed a tree.
I'll teach the basics that you'll need.
I focus more on style than speed.
I'll teach you how to choose a tree
that you can climb successfully.
I'll teach you during trial runs,
which branches are
the strongest ones,
so you will never
have to stop,
until you reach the very top.
And once you're there
you look around and wonder
how you're getting down.
And I could show you
what to do,
but that's
Tree Climbing 102.

Morning Shouldn't Come 'Til Night

"I'm really not a morning person", you've heard people say.
Or "morning simply has to be the worst part of the day".

I've come up with a strategy I think could be a hit.
The trick is finding out a way of implementing it.

The problem with the morning is the getting out of bed,
so if that could be rescheduled another time instead,

then I think you'd find most people would agree without a fight
that the best way is to just delay the morning until night.

Now it needs coordination with the sun and with the moon,
and for us to really pull it off, we'll skip the afternoon.

I haven't got this all planned out, there's parts I'll need to tweak,
but I like to think that we can have this running by next week.

I don't need you to thank me with your cards and gifts and hugs.
I just need you to bear with me as we work out all the bugs.

So the next time that you wake up and you look out at the sky,
don't be surprised if you should see a shooting star go by.

And with sunrise now at nighttime it will sure seem kind of strange,
and it may just take a week or two adjusting to the change.

But the end result of all of this should make it all alright.
If you're not a morning person, now the morning comes at night.

I Saved A Couple Yesterdays

I saved a couple yesterdays
and put them in a box.
I keep them safely stored
beneath my bed.
I'm keeping them for times
when I would like to reminisce
with something more than
thoughts inside my head.

The box is not a big one
so there's only so much room.
I think that's probably
how it ought to be.
I've got some birthday parties
and some holidays and such
and some things that are special,
just to me.

Some yesterdays I saved
might seem unusual to some.
It's not all big events that I replay.
One's a rainy morning when
I still was very young
and I saw my first rainbow on that day.

And that's one of those days
that over time just slips away,
so I kept it and I put it in the box.
It's nice to know I've got a few
that stay just as they were
without the curse of calendars and clocks.

So every now and then
I'll grab the box and pick one out
and I go back and
have that day again.
It's really quite a treat
to take a break from where you are
and spend a little time
with where you've been.

It Wasn't My Idea

Let me start by saying
that it wasn't my idea,
so you can save your "oh my gosh"
and hold your "momma mia".

It started very harmlessly
until somebody said
they thought our team would have good luck
if I just shaved my head.

And then somebody mentioned that
our spirit would show through
if I went out and got myself
a Superfan tattoo.

And then another fella said
I ought to paint my face,
because it isn't every year
we're in a pennant race.

And finally somebody said
if we support this team,
then I should cover my bald head
with gobs of shaving cream.

And people look at me and say
I wouldn't want to be ya.
And I just keep reminding them
it wasn't my idea.

(I Need More Than) A Penny For My Thoughts

A penny for your thoughts
is what somebody offered me,
and I just laughed it off because
I clearly disagree.

I think the going rate
is like a dollar sixty-four.
The penny that was offered
is worth nothing anymore.

I'm really not prepared to
settle for a lesser rate.
You can probably find some cheaper
but the quality's not great.

And any thoughts I give
come with a written guarantee.
"The thoughts that you are getting come
exclusively from me".

So put your money where your mouth is,
that's what I intend to do.
For a measly dollar sixty-four
I'll think a thought for you.

Christmas the Second

Christmas comes but once a year
but I'm suggesting twice.
A second Christmas sometime
in the summer would be nice.

Some snow, some elves, a Christmas tree
oh well, ok I'm lying,
I'm in it for the presents,
you can't blame a guy for trying.

Above The Bottom

As long as you're above the bottom
everything is swell.
There isn't much to getting there,
as far as I can tell.

People tend to tell you
you don't want to be a flop,
and if you work or play real hard
you'll come out on the top .

And if you're not the one on top
and standing very tall,
the bottom seems to be
the very lowest place of all.

The bottom isn't quite as bad
as people like to think.
However, if you cannot swim,
the bottom's where you'll sink.

That doesn't make it good or bad,
but I've learned this so far.
The bottom of a cereal box
is where the prizes are.

Some wind up on the bottom
and some wind up on the top,
and at different times throughout your life
the top and bottom swap.

So sometimes you're the very best
and sometimes, well, you're not.
But if you know you've done your best
that really says a lot.

So if you think the bottom
isn't quite the place to be,
try sitting on your bottom
and I'm sure that you'll agree

that no matter where you find yourself
in all the years to come,
the bottom, top, or in between
there's room for everyone.

Arctic Breath

I love it when the air turns cold
and autumn fades away,
and then sub-zero temperatures
are here most every day.

The reason for my happiness
is when it's cold as death.
I get a chance to look and see
my frigid arctic breath.

I like to watch my breathing when
the air is cold and clear.
It's like I'm making my own clouds
that quickly disappear.

I like to stick my finger through
when I blow frosty rings,
and I imagine using my
ice breath for freezing things.

But this is just a winter sport,
and here is what I think.
If you see your breath in summer, then
your breath must really stink.

Poet Try

I'm working on my poetry.
I think it's going well.
I think I've got the rhyming down
as far as I can tell.

The problem that I tend to have
is this disturbing trend.
My mind begins to wander
when I'm getting near
the part of the poem where you wrap it up and make it all come
together, but instead of just finishing I start to think of all the
other things that I should have included and I start to second
guess myself and then I can't stay focused and I lose my con-
centration, (hey look, a bird), but then I circle back and remember where I was and that I need to simply write
the end

Giraffapotamus

The rare giraffopotamus
is hardly ever seen.

It's not a hippo or giraffe,
it's something in between.

And if you ever see one
please be careful not to laugh.
You'll see the hippo head is on
the neck of the giraffe.

The body is the hippo's
with giraffe legs underneath.
The other most important part
is giant hippo teeth.

They feast on leaves and branches
since they're so high in the air.
You'd think they'd get enough to eat
with all the trees out there.

But why girrafapotami
have trouble being fed,
is since they're so top-heavy
they tip over on their head.

So your best chance to see them
is below the trees with their
heavy heads down on the ground
and butts up in the air.

And with all their trouble eating
if you split them back in half,
you'll have a hungry, hungry hippo
and a skinny old giraffe.

So now you know a bit about
girraffapotamus.
Next time we can talk about
the elenoceros.

Vacuum Cleaning

We had a vacuum cleaner that we used for many years,
it worked well and we liked it very much.
It was just your basic model with a switch for on and off
and a big red button labeled DO NOT TOUCH.

Now the standard on and off switch really covered all our needs,
so that big red button didn't make much sense.
But add a label saying DO NOT TOUCH for all to see,
that's sort of like a dare, in my defense.

It isn't very often that I vacuum, that's for sure
when I finished with my bedroom and the halls
I had to push the button, it's my duty as a kid
and that vacuum sucked the paint right off the walls.

It must have been some kind
of super powered turbo thing.
I bet it was developed by the feds.
I'm not sure what the purpose
of that super-suction is
but it pulled the mattresses
right off our beds.

It pulled the carpet off the floor
it sucked the doorknob off the door
it took the light switch and the lights
it took the desk where papa writes
it got the table and the chairs
it even took a couple stairs
it swallowed up a fireplace log
we still can't find our cat and dog
we think it gobbled mamas blouse
well basically it ate the house.

And I never got an answer
as to what the purpose was
or to why our vacuum
was the special one,
and I never ever pushed that button
one more time again
but I think I'll do it someday just for fun.

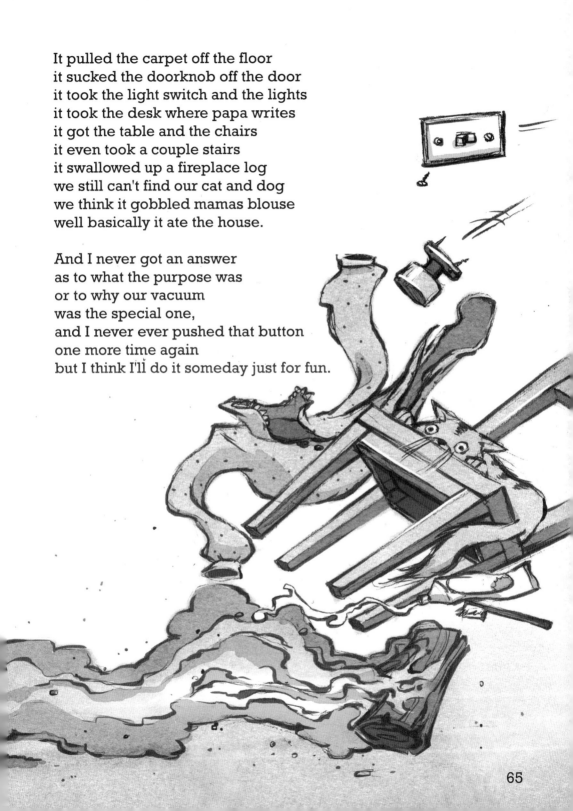

Balloons And Porcupines
Don't Mix

It's really just a basic fact,
not something you can fix,
it's a simple law of nature,
balloons and porcupines don't mix.

The two are not compatible,
and if they would begin
to have a battle, head to head,
you know which one would win.

So if someone cares to make a bet,
and if you're so inclined,
my advice is that you put your money
on the porcupine.

Advice

Here's a little bit of wisdom
I discovered pretty quick.
Never, ever hit a beehive
with a hockey stick.

Banana Splits

A fruit truck had an accident
and dumped its fruits and bits.
I stepped on two bananas
and performed banana splits.

Run For Your Life

They say that running helps your heart
and keeps your body fit,
and any kind of exercise
will have its benefits.

So I am very pleased to start
my exercise routine.
The school bully is after me
and he is mighty mean.

He's sorta like a mountain,
and he's sorta like an ape,
when he walks he drags his knuckles,
and he's kind of out of shape.

But earlier he said to me
"hey kid, give me your lunch,
and if you know what's good for you
you'll save yourself a punch".

I never know what's good for me,
I've always known that's true.
So I said "what's the matter
don't they feed you at the zoo"?

I probably could have saved myself
the trouble and the strife,
but calories burn faster when
you're running for your life.

Bargain?

I bought a nickel for a dime
I think I got a deal.
The nickel's nearly twice as big.
It really was a steal!

Question Mark

Somebody stole a question mark
and no one will confess.
Just who would dream up such a crime
I can't begin to guess.

They brought in the police
who questioned Larry, Sue and Clark,
and lots of other kids but they
forgot to question Mark.

A Most Outstanding Cannonball

I'm famous for a lot of things
but what most folks recall,
is the day I thrilled them with a
most outstanding cannonball.

The day, it was a breezy one,
and hot, no sign of chills.
And like a dope I bragged about
my cannonballing skills.

And bragging comes quite easily,
there's really nothing to it.
The problem's when they call your bluff
and then you have to do it.

So my choices were to tell the truth
and tell them all I lied,
or to give the cannonball a shot,
and try to keep my pride.

It was at the local swimming pool.
The high dive, at the top.
Where the worst thing that can happen
is the dreaded belly flop.

But I blocked that thought out of my mind
and walked out on the board.
I looked down for the judges
but I wasn't being scored.

And a lot of people gathered,
shading eyes and craning necks.
They were like the folks who go
to stock car races for the wrecks.

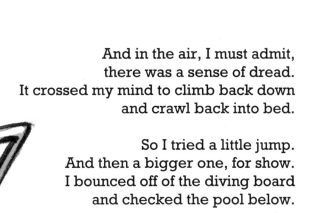

And in the air, I must admit,
there was a sense of dread.
It crossed my mind to climb back down
and crawl back into bed.

So I tried a little jump.
And then a bigger one, for show.
I bounced off of the diving board
and checked the pool below.

I took off in the air
and arched my back and grabbed my knee.
My mind said I should add a flip,
my body disagreed.

I knew that my success (or not)
was based upon the splash.
I concentrated on the pool
while hoping not to crash.

So I waited for the impact
from the water down below,
to see what kind of splash I'd make
and how far it would go.

And then my body hit the pool,
it hit it pretty hard,
but from every indication,
I did well in that regard.

And the pool was nearly empty
from the water I displaced.
The entire pool deck was swamped.
Old records were erased.

And I knew I really nailed it
and my name was cheered by all,
after truly pulling off a most
outstanding cannonball.

Cartwheels Are Overrated

They've found another way for me
to feel humiliated.
'Cause some kids can and some kids can't,
cartwheels are overrated.

It's just a sideways somersault
with a little bit more flair,
but somehow when I try it
I land on my derriere.

I'm trying to adjust my style
and go full speed ahead,
but when I don't land on my butt
I smack my head instead.

If I was meant to spin like that
I would have been a wheel,
and they would just think I need oil
when people hear me squeal.

I think it's just that certain kids
are built to do this stuff
and some of us are meant to watch
and that should be enough.

The problem with the cartwheel is
I just don't really care.
I think I'll work on my handstand
and then I'm halfway there

and I'll feel very satisfied
that I participated,
but I maintain my theory that
cartwheels are overrated.

Crust

They've got to find a use for crust
so much of it goes wasted.
My guess is barely ten percent
is ever even tasted.

I thought I could invent a loaf
without the outer skin,
but found you really need the crust
to keep the bread part in.

Stand Up

I'm breaking into comedy
I might be going pro.
I'm working on my stand up and
I'll do a one-man show.

I've got the perfect suit and tie
I cut and styled my hair
I even hired a vocal coach
to help me to prepare.

It seems that I have all the tools
to make a lot of money.
The only real problem is
I'm just not very funny.

Favorites

Music is my favorite thing
I like to listen to the King
when I hear Elvis then I sing
'cause singing is my favorite thing

and when I sing I like to dance
and shake a bit and move and prance
and really get the room to swing
'cause dancing is my favorite thing

and when I dance I like to drink
and I don't care what people think
it's not like I'm just guzzling
'cause drinking is my favorite thing

and when I drink I have to eat
vegetables, desserts or meat,
I'll stuff my face with anything
'cause eating is my favorite thing

and when I eat I need a nap
a bed, a floor, or someone's lap,
just keep me from awakening
'cause sleeping is my favorite thing

and when I sleep I love to dream
of leprechauns and jellybeans
and plastic flowers blossoming
'cause dreaming is my favorite thing

but in my dream I did some harm
I somehow fell and broke my arm
and now my arm is in a sling
my broken arm's my favorite thing.

Alright, it's gone on long enough
I really don't like all this stuff.
That shouldn't be earth shattering
'cause lying is my favorite thing.

So now it comes as no surprise
I'll face the music for my lies
whatever consequence it brings
'cause music is my favorite thing...

Getting In Shape

I signed up for a membership
down at my local gym,
it's time I got myself in shape
this isn't just a whim.

I started off quite slowly
over time I will improve
and I will sculpt my body like
a statue in the Louvre.

And after just one workout
I can really feel the burn,
in fact I've got some aches and pains
that cause me some concern.

I scraped up my elbow
I twisted my knee
I sprained my left ankle
most definitely.
There's a bump on my forehead
I stubbed my big toe
dropped a weight on my finger
just moments ago.
My foot's got a blister
my muscles feel tight
there's a kink in my neck
and my shoulder's not right
I heard something go bang
and a knuckle go pop
and I felt a bit dizzy
so figured I'd stop
and my workout had lasted
about half an hour
and on top of it all
I fell down in the shower.

So I hope they really mean it
when the say "no pain no gain".
I'll focus on the gain some more
the next time that I train.

The pain, I think I've got that down
that's not the part that thrills me,
but I will get myself in shape
even if it kills me.

The Flute

The trickiest thing
about playing the flute
is bees flying in
when you're trying to toot.

Try Something Gnu

My parents just bought me a gnu for a pet
and I'm not quite sure what to do.
I sort of expected a dog or a cat
but they both said to try something new.

So now that I've got him he stands in the yard
just like he would do at the zoo.
I'd like to try teaching him tricks so I asked
would you like to try something, gnu?

He took to his training as quick as a wink.
I hoped that he would, but who knew?
So now he can fetch and roll over and beg
just like a new gnu ought to do.

We're all very happy with how things worked out
there's nothing that I would undo.
I now knew the gnu was the right pet for me
and I knew that my gnu knew it too.

Gum On My Shoe

I was minding my business and walking to school
concentrating on songs that I hum
and not paying attention to where my feet went
and I stepped in a huge wad of gum.

Now my first gut reaction was scrape it off fast
which is perfectly normal to do,
but I stepped on the grass just before I could scrape,
now there's gum and there's grass on my shoe.

And I thought really quick that I needed a stick
to remove this gross gummy grass mess,
but the stick became stuck; now it's part of the muck,
so that brainstorm was not a success.

I was worried by now that I'd be late for school
and while trying to think this thing through
I stepped on a newspaper there on the ground
which conveniently stuck to my shoe.

So I thought if I hurried my shoe would come clean
so I ran, but I soon found out that
all the gum on my shoe was more like super glue
which was bad since I stepped on a cat.

So I've now got a living thing stuck to my shoe
which is quite an ordeal for a kid.
I was careful to not put my weight on that foot
but I'm sure that a few times I did.

Now my options were few with this cat on my shoe
so I thought I'd go back to my house,
so I spun 'round and hopped and the craziness stopped
'til the cat started chasing a mouse

and the cat ran amuck and the mouse was now stuck
which I had to do something about,
and the right thing to do was to take off the shoe
and let all of this sort itself out.

Trying not to get bit I proceeded to sit
on the ground since there wasn't a chair,
and the shoe was tied tight but I hoped that I might
just untie it and then go from there.

When I tried to unlace the cat hissed in my face
and I think I know what was the matter.
He had gum in his fur and his purr kind of slurred,
and he did seem a little bit flatter.

But I got my shoe free, well, eventually
and decided to bid it farewell
and I thought about that, my shoe, mouse and flat cat
would have made for a great show and tell

but that thought had to wait, I was already late
and I had to explain my delay.
So the boy with one shoe told them, all of it true,
but they shook their heads as if to say

that the truth had been stretched and your story's far-fetched
and it couldn't have happened like that,
so the lesson for me is to walk carefully
and to watch out for gum, mice and cats.

Take Two

I wish life was more like the movies
'cause I often could use one more take.
It would sure come in handy to get one more try
and just simply cut out the mistakes.

Super-Steve

Faster than a speeding bullet
flying through the clear blue sky
stronger than a locomotive
None of those am I.

Protector of our precious planet
known for brains and bravery
gets the bad guys and the ladies
Sorry, that's not me.

But...

If your pocket needs protection
with a custom plastic sleeve
if your fountain pen is leaking
then they call on Steve.

He can work a calculator
crunching numbers 'til they cry
need someone to do your taxes?
Mister, I'm your guy.

Mooseback Riding

People love to horseback ride,
you bet your boots they do.
For me that seems a bit too tame;
I thought of something new.

I thought I'd try a mooseback ride,
so I need to produce
the necessary paperwork and
necessary moose.

A moose license is hard to get,
they're not just on some shelf.
I don't know where you'd get one so
I printed one myself.

And then there is the moose you need
since that's what you will ride.
I wrote the mooseback riding club
to see what they'd provide.

As I waited for an answer
my impatience grew and grew,
so I took the matters in my hands
and stole one from the zoo.

Now I had my troubles the first time I tried
and I don't use this as an excuse,
but half of the challenge of learning to ride
is getting yourself on the moose.

And once you get up there (a ladder can help)
you're not really sure where you are.
You just know it seems like you're five stories high
and the ground down there looks mighty far.

Now the moose isn't really
that thrilled that you're there,
you can tell cuz he's starting to snort,
and shoot snot out of nostrils
that look like two caves,
and you sense that
this ride will be short.

And the grip is a problem since mooses don't come
with handles that somehow appear,
so you grab a big handful of moose fur and hope
that the antlers will help you to steer.

And you brought the supplies
that all moose riders need
like a canteen and good hunting knife.
You make sure your backpack
is strapped to your back
and then you hold on for your life.

Then you kick and you yell and you say giddyup
and prepare to take off like a hawk.
Then you realize that mooses don't like to run,
they just barely bother to walk.

And because I was small and the moose was so tall
he didn't obey my command,
and he kept slowly walking wherever he pleased,
and quite frankly it got out of hand.

So I pushed the right antler to turn to the left,
and the left one to turn to the right,
and I managed to get him back where we began
so my mooseback ride turned out alright.

I'm thinking of seeing how far this can go.
It might even be a career.
There's not many good mooseback riders out there,
and fewer that know how to steer.

Lucky Horseshoe

I've got a lucky horseshoe,
it's been very good to me.

It's given me good fortune
since I found it, luckily.

I'd like to bring it in to school,
to Show and Tell of course.

The problem is the horseshoe is
still fastened to the horse.

Everybody Needs A Nap

I think that everybody in the world could use a nap.
I think they need one every single day.

A little nap to get refreshed and energize the mind,
and make those daily troubles go away.

And also everyone should get to sit in someone's lap,
and that one may be harder to allow.

But first you get a nap, and then you sit in someone's lap.
It worked in kindergarten, why not now?

I'm Running For President

I'm running for President,
don't you agree,
that no one has qualifications
like me?

I'm a very fast runner,
I sing beautifully.
And there's nobody better
at climbing a tree.

I'm a very good listener,
(wait, what did you say)?
And they say that I play
a mean game of croquet.

You can hide something
and I can find where you hid it.
I can burp and make it
look like someone else did it.

And I promise to work hard,
I'm not one who quits,
and to give everybody
free banana splits

and to clean up pollution,
and make each day sunny,
and I promise each voter
a truckload of money

and I promise no taxes,
I promise no wars,
I promise no homework,
I promise no chores.

Now these promises I made
may end up neglected.
I just made them all
so that I'd get elected.

And once I'm in office
I'll say "my intent
was to prove ANYBODY
can be President".

My Ears See How You Smell

I've discovered an unusual
and most amazing thing.
I didn't even wish for it
or rub a magic ring.
It's really quite a story,
though embarrassing to tell.
If I turn slightly sideways
then my ears see how you smell.

It's not a very useful skill
but still it comes in handy
when someone standing next to me
is eating chocolate candy.

I'll tilt my head a little
and my ear becomes a snout,
and I'll say "THAT SMELLS DELICIOUS"
and it kind of freaks them out.

So I'll keep my little secret
so as not to cause a fuss
though it's torture sitting next
to someone stinky on the bus.

Now the thing to be concerned about,
most everyone agrees,
is I'll blow my brains right out my ears
the next time that I sneeze.

So I'll wear two pairs of earmuffs
to prevent a cold or flu
and to keep my brains inside my head the next
time I KER-CHOO!!!

And here's the other part of this
that's creepy, I suppose,
but to tell me any secrets
you must whisper in my nose.

Swimming To The Moon

I've come up with a project that I plan on starting soon.
I've got my fins and snorkel and I'm swimming to the moon.

The people that I tell this to all seem to wonder why
I just don't build a rocket, and instead of swimming, fly.

They make some decent arguments and really seem to care,
and they're very quick to point out I'll be swimming through the air.

And they say that flying is the proper way of getting there,
and that swimming, plainly speaking, is a water-based affair.

But I can't afford a rocket, hey, I'm not a millionaire.
And to tell me I can't do it, well I take that as a dare.

So I'm doing everything that I can think of to prepare.
I've practiced all my swimming strokes and shortened up my hair.

It's just a couple hundred thousand miles so they say,
and I did seven laps around my swimming pool today.

And moving through the water is much harder than through air,
so it's not apples to apples, and you really can't compare.

And up 'til now I'd say the biggest stumbling block I've found
is figuring out which stroke to use to get me off the ground.

But once I have that figured (and I plan to have it soon),
full speed ahead and pretty much a straight shot to the moon.

I plan to use my freestyle and my backstroke and my crawl,
my breaststroke and my butterfly, I'm gonna use 'em all.

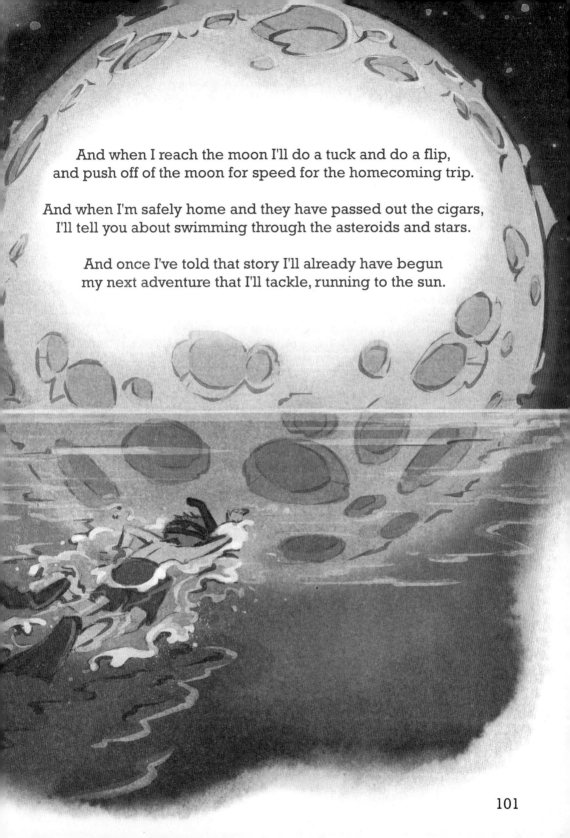

And when I reach the moon I'll do a tuck and do a flip,
and push off of the moon for speed for the homecoming trip.

And when I'm safely home and they have passed out the cigars,
I'll tell you about swimming through the asteroids and stars.

And once I've told that story I'll already have begun
my next adventure that I'll tackle, running to the sun.

I Hypnotized My Dog

I tried to hypnotize my mom
and wound up quite surprised.
It didn't work on mom and yet
my dog got hypnotized.

I don't know how to snap him out,
he sort of stares and snores,
so while I've got him in my spell,
I'll make him do my chores.

Unicornicycle

I bought a unicycle
and I added on a horn
and when I ride it now it's like
I'm on a unicorn.

Pants

These pants have sure seen better days
but pants are like old friends.
You can't just dump or toss them out.
That can't be how it ends.

So maybe both the knees are torn,
the pockets all ripped too.
They're grass-stained, paint stained, patched and
frayed,
they're more or less see-through.

And every time I pull them on
I'm sure that there's no way.
But somehow due to great technique
They last another day.

We've run and jumped and tripped and fell
and climbed and crawled and slid.
We've had such great adventures
it's just awesome what we did.

We've both grown up together
and for every rip and tear,
there's a story or experience
my pants and I both share.

But no matter how you wish and hope
that things could stay the same
there comes a time to move along
and sometimes that's a shame.

I don't think I can save these pants
but every day I try
to make them last just one more day
before we say goodbye.

Take The Mummy and Run

My friends went to Egypt to spend a few weeks
and to travel around and explore
and one day they decided to visit the tombs
just to see what that might have in store.

They were hoping to see an old mummy
or something like King Tut or one of those guys
and they walked down a hall, and there, seven feet tall
there was one right in front of their eyes.

There were signs everywhere saying please do not touch
the exhibits or you will be found
in contempt of the rules and you'll certainly be
prosecuted and thrown from the grounds.

And then one of them touched just the edge of the wrap
and the whole thing began to unwind
and the entire mummy completely unwrapped
like an archaeological find.

There were no other visitors inside the tomb
and no guards to see what had been done
and if they were found out they could end up in jail.
My advice, take the mummy and run.

I Can't Wait For Something

I can't wait for something,
but I don't remember what.
It's got me quite excited
so it must be special, but

I have no recollection
so I'm trying hard to think
I hope it doesn't disappoint,
I hope it doesn't stink.

This thing that I am waiting for
I wish I could recall,
I think I'm going to have to
bang my head against the wall

and try to nudge my brain a bit.
It never failed before.
I really wish I knew
what I was so excited for.

Was it something that I ordered?
Is it something from a friend?
Was it coming in the mail?
Will this mystery ever end?

Oh wait, I think I've got it,
after all this time it took.
The thing I'm waiting for is my
"Improve Your Memory " book.

Cramp City

I love to run, and when I run,
it always seems a pity,
no matter where I'm running to,
I end up in Cramp City.

Cramp City is a place where you
will feel your muscles burn.
Your sides will ache, make no mistake
you won't want to return.

So if you go out for a run,
remember this short ditty.
Just take it slow or you will know
the tortures of Cramp City.

Justin Case

My very dear friend Justin Case
keeps bits and pieces every place
he never, ever throws things out
which leaves a giant mess about.

A piece of string, a broken chair
and many things beyond repair
a single shoe that has no match
a doorknob that won't reattach

a candy wrapper six months old
a brick of imitation gold
an empty bottle of perfume
his place has never seen a broom

an old tin can, a broken bat
a hairball from a sickly cat
a piece of toast, a tire swing
it seems there's one of everything.

His reason is you never know
if you'll need something someday, so
instead of scrambling to replace
he keeps it all here, just in case.

Stairs Confuse Me

I think there should be signs on stairs
to tell which way they go.
I realize they work both ways,
I'm not that dumb, you know.

But if you had "Just Up" stairways,
and other ones "Just Down",
I think we could alleviate
congestion in this town,

and make it safe when people try
last minute stairway dashes.
And also, it would minimize
those ugly stairway crashes.

Nickname

I really want a nickname,
I need something that will stick,
like "The Kid" or "Dude" or "Freight Train",
or "Mister Cool" or "Slick".

So I'm waiting and I'm hoping
but I found out pretty quick,
that you never get a nickname
when your name's already Nick.

I Threw A Rock

A time like this can make you wonder what you ever did
to get you into such an awful mess.
But if you go back to the start and take it step by step,
you'll see the cause of all of this distress.

I threw a rock
that hit a tree
that scared a squirrel
terribly.

The squirrel jumped
(as squirrels can)
and landed on
the mailman

who screamed and took off
down the street
and ran the shoes
right off his feet.

He ran so fast
his shoes got hot.
He thought they'd cool off;
they did not.

And just then
a newspaper blew
and wrapped around
his steaming shoe.

The paper's temperature
went higher
and suddenly
it caught on fire.

And then a gust of wind
blew hard
and blew the paper
toward my yard.

The burning paper
flew my way
and looked like it would
float away,

but landed on my
roof instead
and that is how
the fire spread

to my garage
to be exact
my house was farther
toward the back.

It burned the doors
and walls and then
it burned my dad's
Mercedes Benz.

The firemen came
and saved the rest
but now I'm feeling
rather stressed.

I'm not sure what
to tell my dad.
I'm guessing he'll be
kinda mad.

I must admit,
it's quite a shock
what happens when
you throw a rock.

The Declarations of Jim Dependence

My good friend Jim Dependence said
"Well now, I do declare,
I'd rather shave my beard off
than be eaten by a bear.

And I declare that fingernails
are now worth more than gold.
And I declare that ice cubes
have no business being cold.

And one more declaration
that you probably hadn't heard.
I just declared that cinnamon
is now a dirty word.

I think you get the picture
and it's really kind of sad.
My good friend Jim Dependence
is quite positively mad.

Dilemma

Bud said, "I'll eat anything, what should it be"?
so I dared him to swallow a dollar
and I gave him the change that I had in my pants
and he smiled and he loosened his collar.

And he measured the coins into three little stacks
and he placed them in line on his tongue
and in one fancy slurp he just sucked them all down.
Quite impressive for someone so young.

And Bud smiled the smile of someone who knew
he had clearly impressed the small crowd,
and he topped it all off with a fifty cent burp,
very classy and not very loud.

Now I said eat a dollar, but Bud really ate
more like $1.25 or about,
and I'd like a refund of the difference except
I'm afraid where the change will come out.

The ScareJoe

My buddy Joe and I decided we would build, one day,
a super scary scarecrow that would keep the crows away.

We found a tattered shirt and made him look like he had died.
We gathered up some grass and hay that we could stuff inside.

We got some faded blue jeans and we dressed him like a bum,
and we found a couple two-by-fours that we could hang him from.

And for the head we chose to use a king size pillow case,
and then used magic markers to create a scary face

with scars and blood and pointy teeth and evil looking eyes,
we put it all together and we tried him out for size.

We took him to a cornfield and we hung him there to see
if our scarecrow was effective, if the crows would truly flee.

And within a couple minutes crows were landing all around,
but surprisingly, my buddy Joe was nowhere to be found.

So I can't say that I'm pleased with the results of our scarecrow,
but I think we have a winner if we wanted a scareJoe.

My Legs Don't Like My Feet

I've got a little problem
and I don't know what to do.
This problem is related
to my pant leg and my shoe.

Just the other day
as I was walking down the street,
I made the realization
that my legs don't like my feet.

I know that it may sound as though
I've lost my mind a bit,
but my feet start walking one way
and my legs go opposite.

This problem, as you might expect,
is causing lots of stress
and my knees are stuck
right in the middle of it all, I guess.

So I sort of trip and stumble
as I wander to and fro,
and if we can't work it out
then one of them has got to go.

And my options are quite limited,
it's not like there are tons.
Without my legs my feet would look
like flippers on my buns.

And without my feet my legs would be
more like a pair of stilts,
and I'd wind up falling over
every time one of them tilts.

So I need cooperation,
we all need to have a talk.
Because, to be quite honest
I'm afraid to take a walk.

So I've come to a conclusion
and now this is where it stands.
If my legs and feet just can't agree
I'm walking on my hands.

Jefferey Gigantisocks

Jefferey Gigantisocks, it's quite a funny name.
And if he doesn't like it much,
there's no one else to blame.

For Jefferey, as you will see,
insists on wearing socks,
that if you laid them end to end
would stretch for several blocks.

Now that all by itself is not
a reason, some have said.
The reason for the name is that
he wears them on his head.

And if that weren't enough he
likes to really pull them down
so that the bottoms of the socks
just sort of make a fuzzy crown.

And since the socks are old
and worn he sees right through
the holes and walks around
in bare feet on his naked toes
and soles.

And he won't change
his barefoot ways
no matter what you do,
unless he meets,
across the street,
Pierre Gigantishoe.

The Sun Turns Upside Down

At bedtime, when
the shadows come
the sun turns upside down.
And when I close
my eyes to sleep
the world just turns around.

And in the morning when I have
my cocoa in my cup,
the whole thing just reverses and
the sun turns right-side up.

And all the while the sun is turning
slowly in the air,
both right-side up or upside down,
it's good to know it's there.

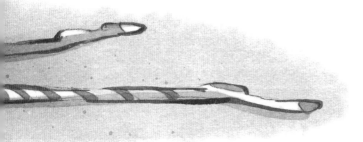

Lost It In The Son

A father had two children
one a girl and one a boy
and each one wanted for themselves
the father's favorite toy

it was kind of like a marble
and was like a prism too
and when held up to the sunlight
rainbow colors would come through

and the children loved to see it
and the colors it displayed
and each wished that they could keep it
every time they looked and played

and each one had a separate plan
to keep it for their own
for they both were selfish children
but the father hadn't known

and one day they couldn't find it
not from where it was before
it wasn't in the normal place
inside dad's dresser drawer

and the father asked the children
and the brother said he knew
what had happened to the marble
and he swore that it was true

then he said "my sister ate it
cause she doesn't want to share"
and the father knew his favorite toy
was gone right then and there

and he thought about his daughter
and the father nearly cried
so he rushed her to the doctor
and he took a look inside

and the doctor said "I see it"
and the doctor got it out
and returned it to the father
who was somewhere thereabout

so they took the marble home
and then returned it to the drawer
and he wasn't sure if he would
show the children anymore

which made the children angry
and just as the father feared
you guessed it, for the second time
the marble disappeared

and the father had a hunch this time
(but hoped he wasn't right)
and he asked his little daughter
there and then that very night

and she said my "brother ate it"
it was just like déjà vu
and the father nearly fainted
but he knew just what to do

so they went back to the doctor
but he said there was no way
to safely get the marble out
so it would have to stay

inside the boy where it would then
remain forevermore
which isn't quite the same as
keeping it inside a drawer

and the father couldn't have it
so nobody really won
he found it in the daughter
but he lost it in the son.

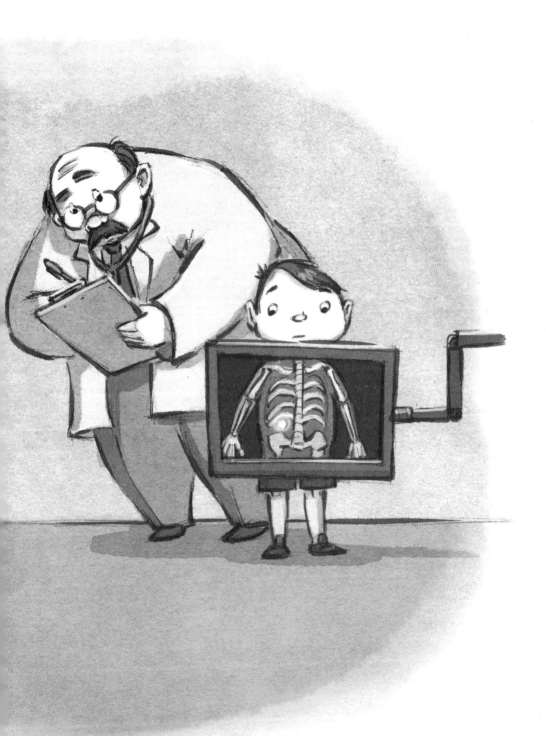

What A Way to Start The Day

Things haven't started very well,
alarm clock didn't ring.
I didn't get my homework done
I haven't done a thing.

I'm sure by now I've missed the bus,
my life's in disarray.
On top of that I'm late for school.
Oh wait, it's Saturday.

Happily Ever...

In most of the fairy tales I've ever known
they all end happily ever after
and all the main characters just carry on
with good fortune, with love, and with laughter.

So my question is why all the misery first?
Save some time since we know what's in store.
And just once I would like to know right from the start
were they happily ever before?

The Tooth Fairy & Me

I've got a good thing going
and it's working perfectly.
We've worked a great arrangement out,
the tooth fairy and me.

I lose a few teeth now and then
and no one really checks 'em.
And for some reason I don't get
the tooth fairy collects 'em.

As if that isn't weird enough,
collecting peoples teeth,
I lift my pillow up and then
THERE'S MONEY UNDERNEATH!

I thought there had to be a catch
or something more to do,
like being someone's butler or
like getting a tattoo.

But strange as it may seem
the deal didn't burn and crash.
I give the fairy teeth and then
the fairy leaves the cash.

Now I can't even start to guess
what use old teeth can be,
but if someone wants to pay for them
then hey, it works for me.

So now I'm branching out a bit,
my teeth are running low.
I need a new supply of teeth
that I can trade for dough.

So if you've got some teeth you're looking
to unload you'll see,
it's a pleasure doing business with
the tooth fairy and me.

Weather or Not

I wake up each morning and turn on the news
and hear all the stories they've got
but then a decision will have to be made
should I watch the weather or not?

The high pressure systems, the graphs and the charts
and all of that technical stuff
confuses me so I just walk out the door
and I figure it out soon enough.

So whether the weatherman's right or he's wrong
whatever the weather may be
the question is whether the weather report
can do any better than me.

Solar Power

I went to the beach one hot 4th of July
you could actually hear the sand bake
and when barefooted people tried walking across
well they practically flew to the lake.

Planting Jellybeans

I planted several jellybeans
outside in our backyard.
I dug holes with a wooden spoon
it wasn't very hard.

I watered them with apple juice
it seemed the thing to do.
I'm waiting for the buds to start
but so far nothing new.

and what I'm really hoping that
this exercise achieves
is jellybeanstalks miles high
with jellybeans for leaves.

And in the fall you'd rake them up
and you know what that means.
You jump into a dream-come-true
a pile of jellybeans.

You eat as much as you can eat
(it isn't like you bought 'em)
then bag the rest to hold you 'til
you start again next autumn.

Holly Looya

The farms were all in need of rain
it hadn't poured all year,
the crops were all in jeopardy
the future was unclear.

So all the people prayed for rain
and asked the clouds to give it,
for this had happened years ago
and they dared not relive it.

But the clouds would not cooperate
they gave no reason why,
so little Holly Looya
planned a mission to the sky.

Now Holly was the bravest
little girl in all the land
and she found a beat up airplane
and she fixed it up by hand

and she took off even though the plane
coughed with an awful sound
and there were those who swore that plane
would never leave the ground.

But they didn't know young Holly
or the courage she possessed
and she flew straight to the clouds
so she could get this drought addressed.

Now the clouds did not appreciate
disruptions to their day,
particularly noisy things
that came from far away.

And she buzzed the clouds and asked them
why they wouldn't send some rain
and they said they couldn't hear her
due to that infernal plane,

and she pushed the plane much harder
and the noise grew so severe
that the clouds agreed to make it rain
if she'd just get out of here.

So she flew away and landed
safely where it all began
as the rain began to pour on down
and drench their desert land.

And the people cheered for Holly
and they ordered a parade
and the put her on their shoulders
and the local brass band played.

Anyone can be a hero
let this be a lesson to ya,
because one was brave the crops were saved
thank the lord and Holly Looya.

Man Oh Man Oh Man Oh Man

I'm trying very seriously
to mind my p's and q's.
And what I mean by that is,
be aware of words I choose.

I tend to have a problem with
expressing what I feel,
so I have taken steps that will
allow me to reveal

when I am feeling frustrated
or mad to the extreme.
If something really ticks me off
and makes me want to scream.

When something rotten happens,
even something quite minute,
instead of saying #$@%**
I simply substitute

a different word or phrase
that is less likely to offend.
It lets me get my anger out
and not have to pretend

that nothing really happened,
this will let me get it out.
And instead of screaming expletives
I take a breath and shout -

MAN OH MAN OH MAN OH MAN
and then I feel at ease.
It helps to calm my frazzled nerves
by varying degrees.

It's making me feel better,
but I think it's only fair
that I find some other trick
to stop me pulling out my hair.

Stu McGrew Got The Flu

"Stu McGrew has got the flu"
I heard our teacher say.
And this is Stu's first absence,
he had never missed a day.

His mom says Stu is never sick,
his system fights it off.
She's never even seen him have
the sniffles or a cough.

The whole thing's very puzzling
although I've got a hunch.
He may have caught the flu bug
because I sneezed on his lunch.

You Think That's Scary

People each have different things
that they consider scary,
like ghosts or being trapped at night
inside a cemetery.

Or being chased by vampires,
and if you think that's scary,
I dreamt I spent the weekend
locked inside the school library.

The Remarkable Story of Hector McTwee

Remarkable stories are told all the time
and some, to a lesser degree,
are only remarkable part of the time
like the story of Hector McTwee.

Now Hector you see, was a genius, and he
had a way of inventing new things.
One day as he tinkered and toyed in his shop
well, he kind of invented some wings.

I say "kind of" because they were covered with fuzz and not feathers
as you might expect.
And they weren't really wings like you'd see on a plane
and their flight-worthiness wasn't checked.

So now Hector McTwee was excited to see
if his wings could take him to the moon.
And although he had never attempted to fly
he was willing to try it, and soon.

And so Hector McTwee got the town to agree
that a moon flight would be a good test.
So the genius named Hector, he strapped on his wings
and he rapidly flapped without rest.

And the flapping he found,
found him still on the ground
and quite hopelessly far from the moon.
So he thought "if I just got a boost I'd be fine".
"I've got it! I need a balloon!"

So now Hector he strapped a balloon to his back
in addition to both of his wings.
And the way that he kept all his flight gear in place
was with stickers and staples and strings.

142

And so Hector McTwee climbed a very tall tree
with his wings and balloon on his back.
And he flapped and he jumped
and he jumped and he flapped
'til the branches were starting to crack.

And with one final spring a remarkable thing
was observed by the crowd down below.
For as Hector was just barely starting to fly
he was grabbed by a giant black crow.

And by giant I mean, not a size in between,
but an actual giant sized bird,
who if measured right then would have easily been
about sixty six feet and a third.

So now Hector WAS flying, though not really trying
to flap anymore since the crow
was the one who was driving, so they'd be arriving
wherever HE wanted to go.

And so Hector may not have arrived at the spot
on the moon that he planned for his route.
But he did get to fly, although not quite as high
as intended when he started out.

And we all hope that space, or a similar place,
is where Hector is going be.
So we watch and we wave and tell tales of the brave
and remarkable Hector McTwee.

Cubes?

Our grandma has a secret ice cube recipe that she
prepares with all her heart and soul and lovin'.
They tend to be quite runny and don't really hold their shape.
I think it's 'cause she bakes them in the oven.

Umbrella

I decided to cut a hole in my umbrella
I did it without any training.
It doesn't quite keep me as dry as it did,
but now I see when it stops raining.

Reverse-A-Goggles

My latest, best invention,
it is something quite unique,
and if you're interested
I can let you take a peek.

They're called Reverse-A-Goggles.
When you put them on your face,
the things you see go backwards
at a most alarming pace.

It's like seeing time unwinding
and it moves by very fast.
You can see things as they used to be
and look into the past.

It's really like a time machine
so I thought, eventually,
if I stare into a mirror
I could see the baby me.

But then I got to thinking,
what if some catastrophe
were to happen with my goggles on
and screw up future me.

Or prevented things to come
because of something that I did.
That's a big responsibility
for such a little kid.

So I thought hard and decided
this was all just too bizarre,
so I put away the goggles 'cause
I like things as they are.

I'm Musically Inclined

I don't play any instruments.
I'm not in any band.
And yet I have a world of sounds
right here at my command.

I whistle like a songbird,
play my nose like a kazoo,
I can burp in several octaves
and I snap quite nicely, too.

I make my mouth go "pop"
by slapping my cheeks with my hand,
and people love to hear me hum.
Yes, I'm in great demand.

And I can keep a perfect beat
by clicking with my tongue.
You see, I'm very talented
for somebody so young.

I play the drums by slapping knees
although it makes them ache.
There really is no limit to
the sounds that I can make.

A trumpet with my armpit
and a toot with my behind.
Though I'm not classically trained
I'm musically inclined.

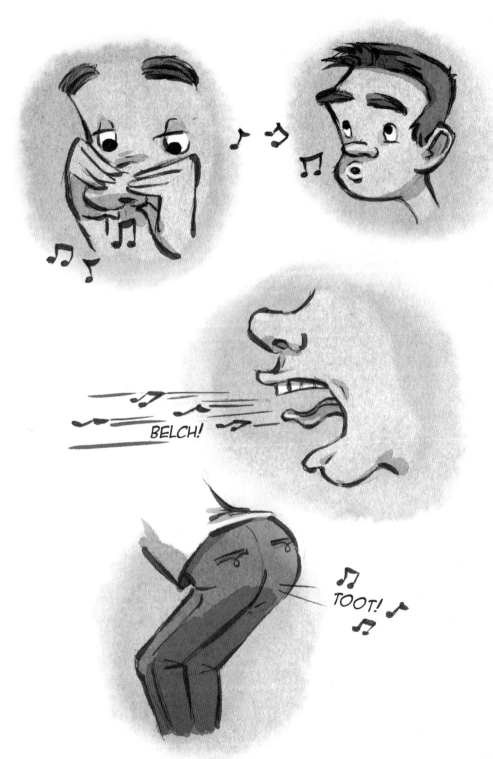

Mixer Licker

I'm the family's mixer licker
so when anybody bakes
I'm the one who gets to sample
batter, frosting, cookies, cakes.

Anytime we use the mixer
my job is my favorite part.
Here's a hint I learned the hard way.
Turn it off before you start.

Did You Ever?

Did you ever use a ladder
just to climb way up a tree
and then jump onto a rooftop
just as graceful as can be

and then climb on up the chimney
and just stand there like King Kong
and beat your chest and yell and scream
(but not for very long)

and then dive off the chimney
towards the tree from where you came
and tumble through the branches
like a human pinball game

and realize that all the while
you thought that you could fly
you're not at all like Superman
you're just a normal guy

and when you finally hit the ground
it's not good what the news is.
They take you to the hospital
with broken bones and bruises.

So did you ever do something
like that, or did you try?
You didn't? You're not quite that dumb?
Oh well, neither did I.

A Sweet Idea

Now candy is one of my favorite things.
I buy most every kind.
The problem is they say it rots
your teeth and rots your mind.

So rather than eating as much as I want
I came up with a thought
to moderate my sweets intake
from all the stuff I bought.

I took all the candy I've been saving up
(I kept it in a jar)
and hatched a plan to melt it down
and make one candy bar.

And all of the flavors would merge into one
that's if I did it right
then I could eat a piece of each
in just one single bite

a chocolate bar
a lemon drop
a licorice whip
a lollipop

a marshmallow
from who knows where
a peppermint
a gummy bear

a piece of fudge
(more like a crumb)
a jellybean
some bubble gum

some candy corn
from at the mall
a candy cane
a sour ball

some taffy
that does not look well
a breath mint and
some caramels

some candy hearts
I bought for fun
a wax mustache
(I'll skip that one).

So this would cut down on the candy I eat
that problem - I erased it
but now the bigger problem is
to find someone to taste it.

Loogie Lou

Here's a tale that's unique
and it's not for the weak,
and I swear that this story is true.
Now before you condemn
the poor boy and his phlegm,
let me tell you about Loogie Lou.

Well the boy was, alas,
voted by all his class,
as the person most likely to spit.
And it's true that he does
but it may change because
he is seriously trying to quit.

Now in case you forgot
about leopards and spots
I'll remind you that some things don't change.
So when Lou comes around
don't stand holding your ground,
I'd advise you to get out of range.

Because Lou is a spitter
and his babysitter
when he was a boy nearly drowned.
For he was a drooler,
a dribbling preschooler,
and nannies would not stick around.

So he never was trained
and the drooling remained
and was never addressed or corrected,
so the boy that we knew
just became Loogie Lou
and continued on being neglected.

But the name seems to fit
and because of the spit
he has never been out on a date.
And I doubt that he will,
well at least not until
he can learn not to expectorate.

Mustache?

I feel my mustache coming in,
and I can see it too.
I touch my upper lip and
I can feel it poking through.

They can grow in very quickly
well, at least that's what I've read.
Looks like brown will be the color
like the hair up on my head.

And it makes you feel much older,
and not quite so immature,
and a beard and sideburns will be
right behind, I'm pretty sure.

And it felt all soft and peachy
and was really smooth as silk,
'til my brilliant mother told me
it was just some chocolate milk.

I Never Saw It Coming

Some people have a sixth sense
and they know when trouble's near,
or they get a certain feeling when
there's something they should fear.

Or when somebody's in danger
or when something's going wrong,
often they can see things coming
'cause their feelings are so strong.

But I do not share that talent
though I really wish I did.
While I wanted to be psychic
guess I'm just a normal kid.

'Cause somebody threw a frisbee
and my sixth sense must be dead.
I never saw it coming
'til it hit me in the head.

stles Don't
und

ndcastles down at the beach.
fancy and tall.
the effort and time
so they're sturdy and won't ever fall.

But no matter the style or adornments or size,
it always ends, to my dismay,
that the tide rushes in with a sand eating grin,
and washes my castle away.

Now it happens this way, every year, every day,
and the point of this pattern, I've found,
is to not get attached cause they're not coming back,
'cause sand castles don't stick around.

So a sand castle then, is a bit like a friend
that you know will be moving away.
You just make the most of the time that you have
and you hope to meet some other day.

There's A Zoo In My Head

I've got this problem that occurs
when I lay down in bed.
It seems that when I'm sleeping
there's a zoo inside my head.

It's not like any zoo you've seen
it's really quite unique.
It's got a dolphin with two legs
and a monkey with a beak.

An alligator with a trunk;
a rhino with some wings,
and a hippopotamus
that plays guitar and sings.

A turtle with a motor
and a polar bear on skates,
and another thing about this zoo;
there are no bars or gates.

It's such a splendid place to be
I sure hope it's not fake.
It's just the kind of place I'd like
to find when I'm awake.

163

My Time Is Running Out

I built a clock with legs so it could walk and move about
but I left the front door open and now time is running out.

Ironing

I wanted to iron a new shirt I bought
the wrinkles were really the worst
it didn't go well 'til I realized it
would be better to take it off first.

The Trampolinist

He was born to his parents, a bundle of joy
a beautiful, bouncing and bright baby boy
from the day he came home people could have foreseen
that his destiny called him to the trampoline.

He bounced on his pillows, the sofa, the bed
and he soon joined the circus where everyone said
he was technically flawless, his flips tight and clean
he was clearly a master on the trampoline.

He'd develop an act that would set him apart
he would make trampolining a true work of art
and he figured this out before he was a teen
and he knew that his future was the trampoline.

He trained night and day at his chosen vocation
and soon he developed a great reputation
as one of the best that the world's ever seen
there was no one more skillful on the trampoline.

And as word spread around the crowds started to grow
with the great trampolinist the star of the show
and the circus attended by kings and by queens
all amazed at his prowess on the trampoline.

All the crowds and the fans wondered what he'd do next
and it's that very question that had him perplexed
he could try different costumes or paint himself green
but there's only so many tricks for trampoline.

And the pressure to add something new to his show
seemed to change him and people saw him undergo
quite a strange transformation, and quite unforeseen
he lost all his interest in the trampoline.

"This is not how I planned this" he said with a smirk,
"what was once my life's passion is too much like work
and I'm only a man, I am not a machine
and I'm tired of bouncing on the trampoline".

Now he knew then and there he had reached his plateau
but he felt that he owed the fans one final show.
In his mind he was already setting the scene
for his final performance on the trampoline.

So he came up with something he hadn't done yet
and he'd leave them with something they'd never forget
just a slight variation to normal routine
made a fitting farewell to the old trampoline.

So the challenge became to jump higher, of course
though he already tended to jump with such force
that the big circus tent couldn't hold him it seemed
for the high-flying master of the trampoline.

Then he asked for some help with a couple of things
and he had all the circus hands tighten the springs
and he didn't feel sad, he was calm and serene
for his final performance on the trampoline.

He started with small hops as he'd always done
and each bounce got more powerful than the last one
'til the top of the tent was all that was between
the heavens and our legend on trampoline.

Then he shot through the top of the big circus tent
it was higher than anyone had ever went
and he landed a mile away in a ravine
as they cheered and tossed roses on the trampoline.

And he never returned and he never looked back
and they fondly remember that memorable act
and it even got mentioned in Time magazine
how he soared like an angel on the trampoline.

And it helped him remember the things he had done
when it wasn't a chore and he did it for fun
and it gave him perspective on what it all means
and he hopes that we all find our own trampolines.

Sooner Or Later

I'm in a skyscraper
whose roof scrapes the sky.
I hear that it's more than
a hundred floors high.

We're going to travel
right up to the top,
where I hear they have
restaurants, restrooms and shops.

I know we'll be getting there
sooner or later,
'cause I pushed every button
on the elevator.

Where Did Summer Go?

I wonder where the summer went,
it seemed to zip right past.
It's one of life's great mysteries,
why school can't go that fast.

Rolling Down A Hill

It's hard to be unhappy
when you're rolling down a hill
it is one of life's great pleasures
and you don't need any skill
you just lay down and start rolling
and you'll slowly pick up speed
as you spin and roll and ramble
like a runaway stampede
and when you reach the bottom
and your barrel roll is done
you've lost your equilibrium
which is really half the fun
and you stand up and you stagger
from the dizziness attack
and you try to get your balance
and it gradually comes back
and you plan another roll and then
you look back up the hill
and you see someone who's up on top
who took a nasty spill
and starts to bounce and roll on down
but hadn't really planned to
and then you think this person is
someone to give a hand to
and in between the screams and shouts
of this poor rolling soul
you see that rolls are only fun
if you had planned to roll.

Senses Gone Amuck

It seems I've lost my senses,
no, I don't mean I've gone mad.
I've lost my taste, touch, sight and sound.
It's really pretty sad.

I've got to get my senses back,
and I'm willing to try
a pinch of pepper up my nose
and lemon in my eye.

It might just shock my system
back to where it used to be,
so I could see and hear and feel
and eat things tastefully.

So here's my plan; to overload
my senses that derailed.
I'll try to wake them up
to where they were before they failed.

So for my nose a bucket of
the worst limburger cheese.
And for my eyes two strobe lights
produced by the Japanese.

And for my ears some headphones
playing loud as they can go.
And for my taste buds, liver,
it's the worst stuff that I know.

But if my plan succeeds
I could get sensory overload.
With all that stimulation
it could make my head explode.

So maybe I'll just go to bed
and hold off on my scheme,
and listen to my common sense
and hope it's just a dream.

Mitt

I'm catcher on our baseball team
our pitcher's really great
he throws the ball so fast
it sizzles right across the plate.

He's got a nasty fastball
he can really bring the heat
it's not much fun to catch it
cause it knocks me on my seat.

My catcher's mitt is wearing out
it burns my hand a bit.
I think I'm going to make a switch
and try an oven mitt.

Odds

They say that there's a better chance of lightning striking me
than winning a big jackpot in the weekly lottery.
Now lightning's pretty random, but the lottery, you pick it,
so what're the odds of being struck by a lottery ticket?

Satisfaction Guaranteed

Make a purchase from our market
SATISFACTION GUARANTEED
everything we sell is perfect,
we've got everything you need.

If you ever have a problem
we'll get on it right away.
We'll take care of any issues
and respond that very day.

We'll send our repairman over
with a hammer and an axe.
We've found most things can be handled
with some pounding and some whacks.

If that doesn't fix your problem
then we go to level two
and we send a specialist
to stop on by and tickle you.

This may seem an odd approach
by now we're sure you're pretty mad
but if our man can get you laughing
then you shouldn't feel so bad.

If somehow that doesn't solve it
then it's up to level three
and our corporate hypnotist
will stop on by if you agree.

He will understand your problem
you will look into his eyes
you'll be feeling very sleepy
and then you will realize

nothing really was the matter
and your purchase was indeed
everything you could have hoped for
SATISFACTION GUARANTEED.

Unfortunate Lee

I'll tell you about an unfortunate lad
whose luck was as bad as can be.
If ever a person was doomed from the start
it was more or less this fellow Lee.

From a very young age these things started out small,
poison ivy or stung by a bee,
but then things escalated and grew more severe,
life did not have a soft spot for Lee.

He was skiing and somehow an avalanche struck,
once he climbed, then fell out of, a tree.
When he tried to go surfing a tidal wave hit.
People didn't hang out much with Lee.

So he went to an island to hope for a change
which of course was a catastrophe
'cause an earthquake had made a volcano erupt
and the lava was headed for Lee.

And he thought," this is fitting, I'll just wait here and
take control of my own destiny
and at least have control of the way I'll go out"
said the very unfortunate Lee.

He assumed that the lava would swallow him up
and just roll him right out to the sea,
but a big bolt of lightning just zapped him and that's
how it ended, unfortunately.

People Don't Believe
What A Liar I Am

I try to tell people I lie all the time.
I tell them, I certainly do.
I think what confuses them most of the time
is that some of my lies might be true.

You think they'd believe me, why wouldn't they, huh?
I've made the point perfectly clear.
The lies I devise come in all shapes and size
and I work hard at sounding sincere.

And if they won't believe
what a liar I am
because of my sweet face
and youth,
then I guess I will have
to confuse them some more
and occasionally tell them the truth.

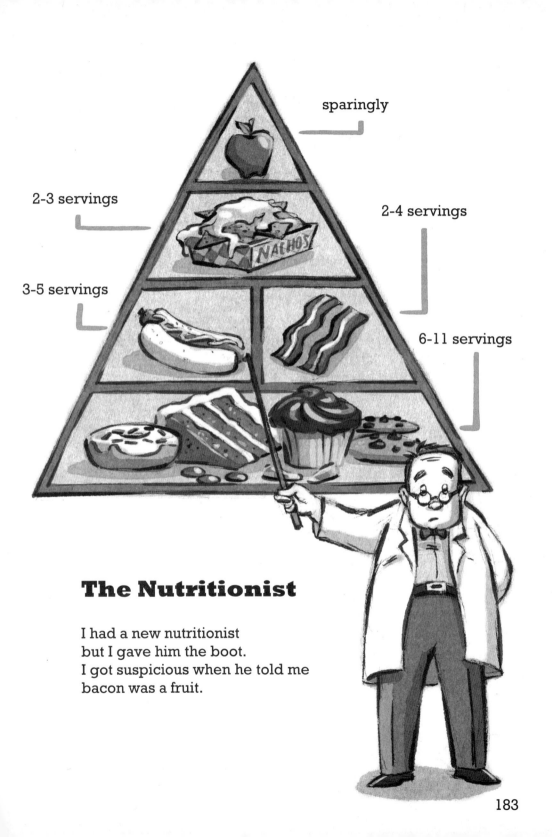

sparingly

2-3 servings

2-4 servings

3-5 servings

6-11 servings

The Nutritionist

I had a new nutritionist
but I gave him the boot.
I got suspicious when he told me
bacon was a fruit.

Robbed

Someone stole my rubber bands
and I don't understand it.
The only explanation is
it was a rubber bandit.

The Grass Is Greener

The grass is always greener
on the other side they say.
I learned it from a kid I shared
a desk with yesterday.
I took a look at pictures
we were coloring all day on,
and all his greens were greener cause
he got the better crayons.

They Only Give You One

Walter lived and then he died
it all went by so fast
and in the end his big regret
was how his time went past.

He lived his life from day to day
and did the best he could.
He did what people told him to
instead of what he should.

He climbed the corporate ladder
because that's what people do
and then he worked much harder
because that was all he knew.

He always tried to get ahead
and never wondered why
but by the time he got there, well,
a lifetime had gone by.

He never had adventures and
he never took a wife
and he didn't do most anything
he wanted with his life.

He didn't smell the roses since
he never really stopped.
Of course he'd like to do that now
but that balloon has popped.

So if there is a lesson here
or something like a riddle,
life is like an Oreo -
the best part is the middle.

Be sure you take time every day
to breathe, and have some fun
and keep in mind you get your time
but there are no reruns.

So use your time as best you can
be happy when you're done
and live your life with no regrets,
they only give you one.

I'd Like To...

I'd like to go outside now but
they say it looks like rain.
I'd like to be a genius
but I haven't got the brain.
I'd like to feel better
when I'm feeling kind of strange.
I'd like to have the answers
but the questions always change.
I'd like to be a millionaire
but I don't have a dime.
I'd like to live forever
but I haven't got the time.
I'd like to tell you something
but I don't know what to say.
I'd like to get to heaven
but I'm not sure how to pray.
I'd like to feel warmer
but I haven't got a coat.
I'd like to sail around the globe
but I don't have a boat.
I'd like to sing a love song
but I haven't got the heart.
I'd like to save the world
but I don't know where to start.
I'd like to buy some furniture
but I don't like to shop.
I'd like to write a poem
but I won't know how to stop.
I'd like to just say thanks for
reading this the whole way through.
I'd like to say I like you
and I hope you like me too.

Index

Above The Bottom, 58
Advice, 67
After You, 32
April May June, 40
Arctic Breath, 60

Balloons And Porcupines Don't Mix, 66
Banana Split, 68
Bargain?, 72
Black And Blue is Nothing New, 34

Cartwheels Are Overrated, 76
Christmas The Second, 56
Cramp City, 109
Crust, 78
Cubes?, 146

Dan Ticipation, 43
Dance Lessons, 42
Declarations of Jim Dependence, 116
Did You Ever?, 153
Dilemma, 117
Dresser, 19
Driving Doesn't Seem So Hard, 44

Escalator Broke, 46
Everybody Needs A Nap, 95

Favorites, 80
Flute, 84
Free Throws, 12

Getting In Shape, 82
Giraffapotamus, 62
Grass Is Greener, 185
Gum On My Shoe, 86

Happily Ever..., 129
Holly Looya, 136
Hot Trick, 29

I Can't Wait For Something, 108
I Don't Have Time To Sleep, 26
I Hypnotized My Dog, 102
(I Need More Than) A Penny For My Thoughts, 5
I Never Saw It Coming, 159
I Once Fell Up The Stairs, 8
I Saved A Couple Yesterdays, 52
I Threw A Rock, 114
I'd Like To..., 188
I'm Musically Inclined, 150
I'm Running For President, 96
Ironing, 165
It Wasn't My Idea, 54

Jail, 14
Jefferey Gigantisocks, 122
Juice Box, 25
Justin Case, 110

Kitchen Dares, 36

Loogie Lou, 156
Lost It In The Son, 124
Lucky Horseshoe, 94

Man Oh Man Oh Man Oh Man, 138
Mitt, 176
Mixer Licker, 152
Mooseback Riding, 90
Morning Shouldn't Come 'Til Night, 50
Most Outstanding Cannonball, 74
Mustache?, 158
My Ears See How You Smell, 98
My Legs Don't Like My Feet, 120
My Shadow Gave Me A Dirty Look, 18
My Super Suction Shoes, 7
My Time Is Running Out, 164

Nickname, 113
Nutritionist, 183

Odds, 177

Pants, 104
Paperboy, 35
People Don't Believe What A Liar I Am, 182
Planting Jellybeans, 134
Poet Try, 61

Question Mark, 73

Remarkable Story of Hector McTwee, The, 142
Reverse-A-Goggles, 149
Rise and Shine, 13
Robbed, 184
Rocket Pilot, 30
Rolling Down A Hill, 173
Run For Your Life, 71

Sand Castles Don't Stick Around, 160
Satisfaction Guaranteed, 178
ScareJoe, 118
Senses Gone Amuck, 174
Shoes Are Gloves For Feet, 38
Shopping Cart Adventure, 20
Snizzles, 48
Snoozin' Susan, 28
Solar Power, 133
Sooner Or Later, 170
Stairs Confuse Me, 112
Stand Up, 79
Sticks And Stones and Broken Bones, 24
Stu McGrew Got The Flu, 140
Sun Turns Upside Down, 123
Super-Steve, 89
Sweet Idea, 154
Swimming To The Moon, 100

Take The Mummy and Run, 106
Take Two, 88
There's A Zoo In My Head, 162
They Only Give You One, 186
This Is Not The Way It Goes, 16
Tooth Fairy & Me, 130
Trampolinist, 166
Tree Climbing 101, 49
Try Something Gnu, 85

Umbrella, 147
Under All This Dirt, 10
Unfortunate Lee, 180
Unicornicycle, 103

Vacuum Cleaning, 64

Weather or Not, 132
What A Way To Start The Day, 128
Where Did Summer Go?, 171

You Think That's Scary, 141